D1175865

The Tragedies of Shakespeare's Antony and Cleopatra

THE TRAGEDIE OF
Anthonie, and Cleopatra.

Actus Primus. Scœna Prima.

Enter Demetrius and Philo.

Philo.
Ay, but this dotage of our Generals
Ore-flowes the meafure: thofe his goodly eyes
That o're the Files and Mufters of the Warre,
Haue glow'd like plated Mars:
now bend, now turne
Office and Deuotion of their view
Vpon a Tawny Front. His Captaines heart,
Which in the fcuffles of great Fights hath burft
The Buckles on his breft, reneages all temper,
And is become the Bellowes and the Fan
To coole a Gypfies Luft.

Flourifh. Enter Anthony, Cleopatra, her Ladies, the
Traine, with Eunuchs fanning her.

Looke where they come :
Take but good note, and you fhall fee in him
The triple Pillar of the world) transform'd
Into a Strumpets Foole. Behold and fee.
Cleo. If it be Loue indeed, tell me how much.
Ant. There's beggery in the loue that can be reckon'd
Cleo. Ile fet a bourne how farre to be belou'd.
Ant. Then muft thou needes finde out new Heauen,
new Earth.

Feeds Beaft as Man ; the Noblenefse of life
Is to do thus : when fuch a mutuall paire,
And fuch a twaine can doo't, in which I binde
One paine of punifhment, the world to weete
We ftand vp Peerelefse.
Cleo. Excellent falfhood :
Why did he marry *Fuluia*, and not loue her?
Ile feeme the Foole I am not. *Anthony* will be himfelfe.
Ant. But ftirr'd by *Cleopatra*.
Now for the loue of Loue, and her foft houres,
Let's not confound the time with Conference harfh;
There's not a minute of our liues fhould ftretch
Without fome pleafure now. What fport to night ?
Cleo. Heare the Ambaffadors.
Ant. Fye wrangling Queene :
Whom euery thing becomes, to chide, to laugh,
To weepe : who euery paffion fully ftriues
To make it felfe (in Thee) faire, and admir'd.
No Meffenger but thine, and all alone, to night
Wee'l wander through the ftreets, and note
The qualities of people. Come my Queene,
Laft night you did defire it. Speake not to vs.
Exeunt with the Traine.
Dem. Is *Cæfar* with *Anthonius* priz'd fo flight ?
Philo. Sir fometimes when he is not *Anthony*,
He comes too fhort of that great Property
Which ftill fhould go with *Anthony*.

he comma in the First Folio title of the play, though unusable as a basis for
rgument, may serve as a symbol of the distinctive treatments given Antony and
leopatra in this monograph. See page 6.

The Tragedies of Shakespeare's Antony and Cleopatra

by

LAURENS J. MILLS

INDIANA UNIVERSITY PRESS

BLOOMINGTON   1964

Indiana University Humanities Series Number 55
Indiana University, Bloomington, Indiana

EDITOR: Edward D. Seeber
ASSISTANT EDITOR: David H. Dickason
ASSISTANT EDITOR: Hubert C. Heffner

The Indiana University Humanities Series was
founded in 1939 for the publication of occasional
papers and monographs by members of the faculty.

PREFACE

IT IS THE purpose of the following monograph on Shakespeare's *Antony and Cleopatra* to determine and describe the tragedy of Antony and the tragedy of Cleopatra. A rather minute analysis of pertinent parts of the play's text forms the basis for the conclusions that are reached. And it is *as a play* that *Antony and Cleopatra* is viewed, not as history or politics or poetry or metaphysics or any other aspect suggested by the drama. Occasional indications that the dramatist kept the audience well in mind will be cited.

Antony and Cleopatra is complex in action, roving in setting, and—a thing that would not disturb an Elizabethan audience—neglectful of strict time designations within the period of Roman history that it covers. It offers in the main a spectacle, not Hamlet-like self-examination. It leaves to the audience the perception of total effects and the realization of the tragic consequences to Antony and Cleopatra brought about by their behavior in the play.

The edition of the text by G. L. Kittredge (1941) is used for citations and quotations. With some modifications the chapter on Cleopatra's tragedy is reprinted, by permission of the editors, from the *Shakespeare Quarterly,* XI (1960), 147–162.

CONTENTS

The Tragedies of Shakespeare's Antony and Cleopatra

❧ ❧

❧ I ❧

Two Tragedies

INTERPRETATIONS of Shakespeare's *Antony and Cleopatra* have emphasized, with varying degrees of stress, one or another of the three principal themes in the play, which are, as summarized by John Munro: ". . . first, the East represented by Egypt and lands beyond versus the West represented by Rome; secondly, the strife in the Triumvirate who divided and governed the world, and the reduction of the three, Octavius, Lepidus, and Antony, to one, Octavius; and thirdly, the love and tragedy of Antony and Cleopatra. Of all these the last is dramatically dominant." [1] But among the commentators who regard the third theme as dominant there is much difference of opinion. Some write as if the play were entitled "The Tragedy of Antony"; for example, J. Middleton Murry: ". . . up to the death of Antony it is from him that the life of the play has been derived. She [Cleopatra] is what she is to the imagination, rather in virtue of the effects we see in Antony, than by virtue of herself. He is magnificent: therefore she must be. But when he dies, her poetic function is to maintain and prolong, to reflect and

[1] *The London Shakespeare,* ed. John Munro (New York, 1957), VI, 1213.

[3]

reverberate, that achieved royalty of Antony's." ² Others give Cleopatra more significance but yet make Antony central, as does Peter Alexander, who allots to Cleopatra a somewhat more distinct, more nearly self-contained personality than does Murry: "Antony dies while the play has still an act to run, but without this act his story would be incomplete. For Cleopatra has to vindicate her right to his devotion." ³ Any interpreter, however, who concentrates on the tragedy of Antony is confronted with the difficulty pointed out by Robert Speaight: ". . . if you are thinking in terms of Antony's tragedy alone, and if you are trying to make his tragedy conform to a classical definition, then you may find it awkward to face a fifth act, in which only his heroic and fallen shadow is left to keep Cleopatra company." ⁴

Judicially objective critics have granted Cleopatra more stature as a tragic figure in her own right than those who think of the play as Antony's tragedy. J. W. Mackail, for instance, though he does not point out that Cleopatra's tragedy differs from Antony's, says: "It is the tragedy not of the Roman world, but of Antony and Cleopatra: and of both of them equally. . . . Here, neither single name gives the central tone to the drama; Antony does not exist for the sake of Cleopatra (as one might put it), nor does Cleopatra exist for the sake of Antony: they are two immense and in a sense equivalent forces which never coalesce, and the interaction between them is the drama." ⁵ And Virgil K. Whitaker,

---

² John Middleton Murry, *Shakespeare* (London, 1936), p. 372.
³ Peter Alexander, *Shakespeare's Life and Art* (London, 1939), p. 178.
⁴ Robert Speaight, *Nature in Shakespearian Tragedy* (London, 1955), p. 123.
⁵ John W. Mackail, *The Approach to Shakespeare* (Oxford, 1931), p. 90.

[4]

though insisting that "the tragic action of the play is centered upon Antony, who has so yielded himself to the passion of love that it has possessed his will and dethroned his reason," gives Cleopatra stature as a tragic figure: "Cleopatra, although she is developed almost as fully as he is, remains the seductress, and only at the end does she become a participant in a tragedy of her own." [6]

Such divergences as these in the views of critics have their origin ultimately in the fact that the story of Antony and Cleopatra as told in Shakespeare's source, Plutarch's *Life of Marcus Antonius,* hardly lends itself to dramatization as a tragedy of two principals with simultaneous catastrophes such as *Romeo and Juliet.* That fact Shakespeare obviously perceived. He was confronted with the problem of writing a play with two central tragic figures whose fates are separated by a time interval and distinguished by different causative forces, while at the same time providing dramatic unity. His solution of the difficulty was to present each protagonist with his or her own character and situation but with personal characteristics and actions that make the two catastrophes heighten each other. The needed unity is provided by the dramatist's making it possible, even obligatory, for the audience to realize and to be constantly aware of the impact of the two catastrophic situations on each other, so that the fate of Cleopatra is foreshadowed by that of Antony and the tragedy of Antony is vividly remembered while that of Cleopatra is in enactment. To create the two-in-one effect and at the same time have the tragedy of each person result from that person's character (and all the while following substantially Plutarch's account) was a remarkable accomplishment.

[6] Virgil K. Whitaker, *Shakespeare's Use of Learning; An Inquiry into the Growth of His Mind and Art* (San Marino, 1953), p. 315.

One very curious fact exists. The title of the play as it appears in the First Folio is: "The Tragedie of Anthonie, and Cleopatra." In view of the apparently chaotic punctuation practices in the early seventeenth century it is not safe to hang an argument on a comma by insisting that the comma in the Folio title represents Shakespeare's or an editor's notification that the ensuing play presents the individual tragedies of two protagonists. Yet if that comma arrived there merely by chance or whim it is an astonishing accident or coincidence. (There is none in the title of *Romeo and Juliet* or of *Troilus and Cressida*.) But the nature of the play *Antony and Cleopatra,* really in itself more than from the comma signal but, if you wish, given added emphasis by it, should be self-evident: the play presents first the tragedy of Antony and then the tragedy of Cleopatra, with each tragedy giving significance to the other and increasing its poignancy and thereby providing a unified tragic effect to the play as a whole.

Tracing the causes of the two tragedies and analyzing the forces that bring them about make it necessary to treat each protagonist separately, though there will be occasional repetition and some glancing, while one character is being discussed, at traits and actions of the other that bear on that other's tragedy. First the tragedy of Antony.

⋖§ II §⋗

Antony's Tragedy

I. ANTONY IN ROME

PHILO SAYS to Demetrius, sadly, regretfully, but penetratingly,

> Sir, sometimes when he is not Antony
> He comes too short of that great property
> Which still should go with Antony.
>
> (I. i. 57-59)

When is Antony "not Antony"? It is when he is in the presence or under the influence of Cleopatra. Apart from her and her influence he exhibits "that great property" (the inherent qualities that are his individual, distinctive characteristics) which, Philo asserts, he should always maintain.

When Antony in Alexandria receives news of the events at home and in Asia (I. ii. 92-107), awareness of his "faults," realization that he *is not Antony,* causes him to say, to himself,

> These strong Egyptian fetters I must break
> Or lose myself in dotage.
>
> (I. ii. 120-121)

And again, after the news of Fulvia's death: "I must from this enchanting queen break off" (I. ii. 132). His word "enchanting" is a confession that Cleopatra exercises a spell on him, a charm. The only way to be free from its influence is to *break off,* to leave Alexandria and attend to his Roman responsibilities and opportunities. He makes an immediate decision, and calls Enobarbus, to whom he says, "I must with haste from hence." He details to Enobarbus the cogent reasons (I. ii. 186–201), and instructs him to deliver orders for departure to "such whose place is under us." Enobarbus' terse "I shall do't," though actually as impersonal as a sailor's "Aye, aye, sir," undoubtedly concurs with his heartiest wishes.[1]

Inasmuch as there exists no real necessity for Antony to list to Enobarbus his reasons for returning to Rome, his explanation not only shows his personal regard for Enobarbus but also forms a rehearsal of the speech he will make to Cleopatra when he goes to her to "get her leave to part." For he is too courteous, too much a gentleman, to think of leaving a queen's court without the formality of asking permission. As he outlines to Enobarbus the "cause of our expedience," his topics are: (1) the death of Fulvia; (2) letters from his friends at home begging him to return; (3) the threat of Pompey and the danger to the state from the people's siding with Pompey. Of these reasons the third is the most important (given the climactic spot in the series); it shows Antony the Roman assigning primacy to business and matters of state.

When Antony goes to Cleopatra (sc. iii) he is immediately

[1] See Appendix I.

the victim of a double cross. Cleopatra had sent Alexas to find him:

> See where he is, who's with him, what he does.
> I did not send you. If you find him sad,
> Say I am dancing; if in mirth, report
> That I am sudden sick. Quick, and return!

Her conversation with Charmian symbolizes the passage of time during which Alexas presumably has found Antony, perceived him to be serious ("sad"), and reported to him that Cleopatra is "dancing." Thus Antony expects Cleopatra to be in good humor. But when he comes to her, she is, as she informs the audience, "sick and sullen." From his expression and bearing she divines his intention, and begins her frustrating behavior. Through her interruptions, taunts, and accusations she completely upsets his plans. After six frustrated attempts to speak he demands that she listen to him: "Hear me, Queen." He cites the "strong necessity of time" that "commands / Our services awhile." But her behavior has had an effect, and in an effort to appease her he says, "my full heart / Remains in use with you." And he postpones until the last the mention of Fulvia's death, which, he says, "most with you should safe my going." The rearrangement has been caused by Cleopatra's tirades; that it is not a preconceived rearrangement is evidenced by the irony in Cleopatra's "What says the married woman?" (l. 20); the question would lose dramatic effect if it were not apparent that Antony is trying to say something about Fulvia.

But the announcement sets her off on another round of tirades, fiercer than the previous; she angers Antony and he turns to go away: "I'll leave you, lady." Subtly, with a rare compliment to Antony's inherent courtesy, though she uses the compliment for her own selfish ends, she causes him to halt: "Courteous lord, one word." She pretends to have something to say, something that she has now forgot.[2] Her appeals to his pity, however, do not divert him from his purpose, for he has recognized her maneuvers. Yet he has been influenced, as his antithetical, paradoxical final speech shows:

> Our separation so abides and flies
> That thou, residing here, go'st yet with me,
> And I, hence fleeting, here remain with thee.
>
> (I. iii. 102–104)

And thus, to a certain extent, Antony has failed to be *Antony* in Philo's terms; he has been influenced by Cleopatra, who has been shrewd enough to take advantage of one of his personal qualities, his courtesy, to wrest a partial victory out of defeat.

In her last speech of the scene Cleopatra has acknowledged the truth in Antony's indirect accusation of "idleness," begged forgiveness, appealed for pity, and, since he is determined to go, wished him success. Antony's "Our separation" speech, contrasting with his "I must from this enchanting queen break off," prefigures his later yieldings to Cleopatra; it is his first failure to cast off completely the spell of the Egyptian charmer.

A second failure is denoted by the pearl that Antony, now in Rome, conveys to Cleopatra by Alexas (I. v.); some concession is implied in that. Cleopatra dispatches messengers to Antony daily; there is only one response by Antony cited. Cleopatra's sending Alexas suggests that other emissaries have failed. Antony's message, as reported by Alexas, is hardly an affectionate love-protestation (and Alexas' hesitancy in repeating it—"His speech sticks in my heart"—

---

[2] See below, p. 37.

shows his awareness of that); its contents reveal Antony's understanding of what may appeal to Cleopatra—power and bounty (cf. V. ii. 86–88)—and tend to reconcile her to his present activity:

> Say the firm Roman to great Egypt sends
> This treasure of an oyster; at whose feet
> To mend the petty present, I will piece
> Her opulent throne with kingdoms. All the East,
> Say thou, shall call her mistress.

> (I. v. 43–47)

Probably Alexas has reported Antony's behavior in the most favorable light, especially his stress on Antony's kissing the pearl; but his description shows that "the firm Roman" is concentrating on his business in Rome, for Antony, Alexas says, "soberly" mounted his steed, whose eagerness for action, concurrent with Antony's, is implied by "high" neighing.[3] But here again, it seems, it is Antony's courtesy that prompts his response.

In both instances of failure to break off completely with Cleopatra, Antony's speech and behavior imply appeasement. From the point of view of Antony's potentialities his concessions, wrested from him by the persistent siren, are unfortunate, and they create uneasiness about his future. But they do not provide any precedent or warrant for supposing that in the ensuing session with Octavius, Antony is hypocritical, anything but firm and genuine. In that session he is Antony at his best.

At the home of the timorous Lepidus, Antony and Ventidius enter the council room together. Antony is wholly occupied with thoughts of Roman affairs, as his *in medias res*

---

[3] Contrast this with Cleopatra's imagined thoughts and pictures of Antony in Rome (I. v. 18–25).

remark to Ventidius (or to himself) shows: "If we compose well here, to Parthia" (II. ii. 15). Lepidus addresses both "noble partners," beseeching that they "Touch . . . the sourest points with sweetest terms, / Nor curstness grow to th' matter" (II. ii. 24–25). Any disquieting effect of his inept plea, born of anxious concern, is tactfully neutralized by Antony's addressing Caesar with "Were we before our armies, and to fight, / I should do thus," though just what behavior—hand-shaking, embracing, or other action—induces the *"Flourish"* of the stage direction is not specified. Antony's "Were we before our armies, and to fight," is obviously emphatic: *Even* were we (you and I, Caesar) about to fight each other; the implication is that they are not going to quarrel, and so Antony's statement is peace-making and conciliatory.

Without other recognition of Antony's polite remark Caesar says "Welcome to Rome." But that simple greeting is not without significance. Since Caesar's residence is at Rome, he is, in a sense, with Lepidus, host to Antony, though Antony is as much Roman as he; yet Caesar may be implying that Antony would be welcome back in the Roman fold, with a subtle innuendo as to Antony's life away from Rome. After Antony's "Thank you" Caesar's "Sit" seems curt. Antony apparently feels that to obey what sounds like an order is an admission of inferiority, and he counters with "Sit, sir." Grudgingly, with "Nay, then," Caesar accedes, and sits down, first or perhaps simultaneously, thus yielding to Antony. Antony has won the first round; he has not allowed himself to be placed in the position of an offender called up on the green carpet. He has "answered like himself" in the minor but significant little contest. It is effective dramatically; it is an instance of double meaning where a seemingly simple situation with a reason of its own for existing—mere courtesy—has another, and far deeper, meaning: the contest for priority in rank and for preëminence.[4] Close analysis of the ensuing conversation is revealing.

Antony proceeds immediately to hold the advantage he has gained; without allowing Caesar to begin carping, he says:

> I learn you take things ill which are not so,
> Or being, concern you not. . . .
>   My being in Egypt, Caesar,
> What was't to you?
>
>   (II. ii. 29–36)

"No more than my residing here at Rome / Might be to you in Egypt," Caesar replies, but he adds,

>   Yet if you there
> Did practise on my state, your being in Egypt
> Might be my question.

When Antony demands that he explain the sinister "Did practise," Caesar cites the wars Fulvia and Antony's brother Lucius made on him, and accuses Antony of provoking the trouble. Antony denies that he had anything to do with that and gives as evidence the testimony of Caesar's own men

[4] M. R. Ridley, *Antony and Cleopatra,* "Arden Shakespeare," rev. ed. (Cambridge, Mass., 1954), p. 52: "Steevens and Johnson both detected in this interchange a resentment on Antony's part at Caesar's arrogating to himself the right to give Antony his gracious permission to be seated. But surely Malone was right in seeing in it no more than an exchange of 'After you' courtesies, which Caesar, anxious to get on with business, terminates by yielding." But Caesar's blunt "Sit" hardly sounds like "gracious permission." The following non-scholarly pronouncement applies perfectly here: "To a man trying to grab the offensive and hold it, it's a comedown to accept an invitation to be seated." Rex Stout, *Man Alive,* Chap. XIII.

(II. ii. 46–48). He then adds the weight of logic, in the shape of an informal syllogism, which formally would be: *Major premise:* You and I have the same cause (being partners in governing the Roman world and keeping the peace); *Minor premise:* Lucius waged war against you; *Conclusion:* Lucius therefore made war against my desire and prejudiced you against me (II. ii. 48–51). His conclusion really is that Lucius did him, Antony, as much harm as he did Caesar, and that therefore he, Antony, could not have had anything to do with the war.

Antony's self-control is shown when Caesar next accuses him of praising himself by "laying defects of judgment" upon him (Caesar) and of patching up his excuses. He thus charges Antony with employing an *ad personam* argument. Instead of retorting to Caesar's own *ad personam* attack, Antony emphasizes the syllogism:

> I know you could not lack, I am certain on't,
> Very necessity of this thought, that I,
> Your partner in the cause 'gainst which he fought,
> Could not with graceful eyes attend those wars
> Which fronted mine own peace.

> (II. ii. 57–61)

By his "very necessity" Antony relies altogether on logic; Caesar has not denied the major premise, and the minor premise is the very fact that Caesar complained about; the conclusion is then undeniable. As to the part taken by Fulvia, her uncurbable spirit was to blame and he, Antony, "could not help it."

Caesar gives no indication that he has been beaten on this point; he now charges Antony, "rioting in Alexandria," with mistreating his messenger. Antony's answer,

> Sir,
> He fell upon me ere admitted. Then
> Three kings I had newly feasted, and did want
> Of what I was i' th' morning; but next day
> I told him of myself, which was as much
> As to have ask'd him pardon,
>
>   (II. ii. 74-79)

cites discourtesy on the part of Caesar's messenger and describes what was as near an apology on Antony's part as was warranted. Actually, Antony implies, in feasting three kings he was attending to business as the Triumvir in charge of the East, though he does not explain—nor does he need to explain—the mission of the three kings. Thus Antony mildly, logically, refuses to be drawn into any rejoinder to Caesar's accusation of dereliction.

Again Caesar, with no sign of acceptance or rejection of Antony's explanation, proceeds to another charge: that Antony has broken his oath to send him aid when needed. Antony qualifies by his "Neglected rather," an admission and a denial: an admission that he did not send arms and aid; a denial that he wilfully broke his oath. He ascribes the neglect to "poisoned hours," which is as close to an acknowledgement of moral delinquencies as he ever comes. He apologizes for that, and for Fulvia's actions, to the extent that his greatness and his honor will allow. It is clear that he will not humble himself in abject submission to the much younger, censoriously inclined Caesar.

Thus ends the series of charges and answers. If Caesar hoped to humiliate Antony, he has failed utterly. But despite the differences in their "conditions" he needs Antony's help and, though having doubts about their remaining "in friendship," expresses a wish for a "hoop" which "should hold us staunch" (l. 117), thereby giving the cue to Agrippa to introduce the suggestion that Antony marry Caesar's sister. After cautious inquiries on both sides the union is agreed upon; Antony with fervent speech,

> May I never
> To this good purpose, that so fairly shows,
> Dream of impediment

(even dream, as the trochee denotes), clearly thinks of this marriage as insuring the absolute break with Cleopatra. He immediately turns to the military problem at hand: "Haste we for it." "Yet," he says, "ere we put ourselves in arms, dispatch we / The business we have talk'd of" (II. ii. 168–169).

While they are dispatching that business, the interview with Octavia, there is the conversation of Enobarbus with Agrippa and Maecenas that contains the description by Enobarbus of the meeting of Antony and Cleopatra on the Cydnus and his declaration that Antony will not leave her "utterly" (II. ii. 238). It is that prediction, as well as Antony's "I will to Egypt" (II. iii. 38), that has led many commentators to accuse Antony of hypocrisy and double-dealing with Caesar and Octavia.[5]

---

[5] E.g., Paul Stapfer, *Shakespeare and Classical Antiquity,* trans. Emily J. Carey (London, 1880), p. 389: "Shakespeare's Antony, faithful to Cleopatra with romantic devotion, has no intention of letting his marriage with Octavia be other than a purely political matter." Or Willard Farnham, *Shakespeare's Tragic Frontier: the World of His Final Tragedies* (Berkeley, 1950), p. 187: ". . . to Octavia he confesses an ill-regulated past life and promises reformation, only to declare himself, when she has left him and he has had an opportunity to talk with the soothsayer, that he will return to Egypt and its pleasures. The Antony of *Antony and Cleopatra,* like the Antony of *Julius Caesar,* can cloak dishonesty with plausibility."

But the real significance of line 10 of scene iii, "Now, sirrah, you do wish yourself in Egypt?" (addressed to the Soothsayer) has usually been overlooked. Antony has been through an emotion-trying experience. The session with Caesar has necessitated strict control of himself and the exercise of logic and reason; Antony has remained calm and courteous, but has been firm; he has kept his dignity despite Caesar's attempts to put him on the submitting defensive. He has met the unexpected proposal that he marry Octavia with equanimity and with no hint of mental reservation. There follows immediately the interview with Octavia the ending of which is given in the first lines of scene iii with Antony's

> My Octavia,
> Read not my blemishes in the world's report.
> I have not kept my square; but that to come
> Shall all be done by th' rule. Good night,
>   dear lady.
>
>   (II. iii. 4–7)

As he leaves the conference and Octavia he is confronted with the Soothsayer, who obviously represents Cleopatra's interests.[6] Antony's "Now, sirrah, you do wish yourself in

---

Frequently, in comments on Antony, critics use the term "political marriage" or some equivalent with the implication that Antony is intentionally hypocritical, as in the following: "Then in Rome Antony makes his second marriage 'for his peace' with Octavia. . . . it is done out of policy from merely prudential (political) motives." G. S. Griffiths, *"Antony and Cleopatra,"* in *Essays and Studies . . . English Association,* XXXI (1946), 40.

[6] Cf. Plutarch: "With Antonius there was a soothsayer or astronomer of Egypt." So Shakespeare is not thinking of a Roman soothsayer. Nor can Plutarch's statement be cited as evidence that Antony was responsible for the Soothsayer's being in Rome. See Appendix II, last paragraph.

Egypt?" indicates definitely that everything is settled, that the Soothsayer may as well go home, that all he represents is in the past and ended as far as Antony is concerned. That question, unfortunate as the consequences prove it to be, shows that Antony has been sincere in agreeing to the marriage, that in fact for him the union with Octavia makes final the breaking off with Cleopatra. Antony should have made the question merely rhetorical and passed on. But he stays, and allows himself, by asking the question "Whose fortunes shall rise higher, Caesar's or mine?" (II. iii. 16)— a question that reveals Antony's thinking about Roman affairs, not Egyptian, and his own future—to become subjected to the Soothsayer's canny flattery and suspicion-arousing comparison:

> Thy daemon, that thy spirit which keeps thee, is
> Noble, courageous, high, unmatchable,
> Where Caesar's is not; but near him thy angel
> Becomes a fear, as being o'erpower'd. Therefore
> Make space enough between you.
>
> (II. iii. 19–23)

Even then Antony rebukes him: "Speak this no more." Yet the Soothsayer, wedging in with "To none but thee," continues, arguing factitiously on the basis of luck, not reason, and carries out his mission, shrewdly realizing that Antony, though exultant, may be fatigued and thus be subject to emotional reaction. Antony ceases to be controlled by logic; emotion supersedes reason, otherwise he would recognize that his superiority to Caesar in the reconciliation scene was disproof of the charge that he is afraid of Caesar. That Antony adduces, to himself, illustrations of the Soothsayer's emphasis on Caesar's better luck, illustrations (from dicing, cock-fighting, quail-fighting) that prove nothing as to military prowess or political ability, reveals the degree of reaction from his previous mental and emotional control. The depth of that descent is marked by Antony's sudden

> I will to Egypt;
> And though I make this marriage for my peace,
> I' th' East my pleasure lies.
>
> (II. iii. 38-40)

It is logical to conclude that it is reaction, not a settled, permeating intent, that produces what Henry David Gray calls the *amazing* "I will to Egypt," [7] nor is it necessary to wonder, as Gray does, whether "the Soothsayer portion of this scene must somehow have got out of place, that perhaps Shakespeare originally put it at the end of this act." [8] Yet Gray is warranted in doubting that Antony has planned a "second infidelity": "That Antony, immediately after what he has said to Octavia, and before he is even married to her, should turn with his nonchalant "I will to Egypt" to plan his second infidelity in advance comes to me like a slap in the face. We cannot believe that he is insincere in what he says to her; there is nothing of that tone in his gratuitous assurances." [9] Furthermore, that the "I will to Egypt" speech reflects momentary reaction rather than a determined intention is shown by Antony's behavior later. When (III. ii) with Octavia he leaves Rome for the East, the area for which he is responsible, the farewell to Caesar gives no hint of mental reservation or hypocrisy on Antony's part. And when, obviously some time later, trouble does arise (III. iv), it is not because of Egypt; it is a conviction on Antony's

[7] "Antony's Amazing 'I will to Egypt,'" *Modern Philology,* XV (1917-18), 43-52.

[8] Ibid., p. 46.

[9] Ibid., p. 45.

part that Caesar has been injuring him and slighting his honor. He has *not* returned to Egypt. But after Octavia sets out for Rome, he does go to Egypt and Cleopatra; he can engage Egypt and her allies on his side (shown by the presence of Cleopatra's fleet at Actium); and, it must be supposed, he has never really forgotten the Egyptian queen.

But to read into the scenes when Antony is in Rome what is not present in the text of the scenes portraying Antony in Rome is both illogical and unfair.[10] The doing so is the basis for the numerous references by critics to Antony's "political marriage" and for implications of tongue-in-cheek double-dealing. Most extreme is Bradley's positive statement, which unjustifiably makes of Antony a liar and a cad: "Nor has he either the patience or the steadfastness of a born ruler. He contends fitfully, and is prone to take the step that is easiest at the moment. This is the reason why he consents to marry Octavia. It seems the shortest way out of an awkward situation. He does not intend even to try to be true to her." [11] More objective but yet somewhat misleading is the comment by E. E. Stoll:

. . . the change in Antony, whereby he deserts Cleopatra and takes up with Octavia, and then to Cleopatra returns, is treated externally, with no explanation whatever. For his return to Cleopatra, indeed, there is ample preparation, in Enobarbus's prediction before and after his marriage to Octavia, and in the soothsayer's warning, which serves Antony for excuse. But in the warning there is no analysis at all, and in Enobarbus's words only an analysis of the charms of Cleopatra. One wonders, not so much at his desertion of the Roman lady as at his marriage to

[10] See Appendix II.
[11] A. C. Bradley, *Oxford Lectures on Poetry* (London, 1909), p. 296.

her; but the whole psychological transaction, which for Racine would have furnished forth the play, stands undisclosed.[12]

Actually the reasons for Antony's leaving Cleopatra and returning to Rome are clear and ample; and it is hardly logical to say that the Soothsayer's warning "serves Antony for excuse," because clearly considerable time elapses before Antony returns to Cleopatra, and then it is largely the result of the situation for which Caesar was somewhat responsible. Octavia makes no complaint either to her husband or to her brother of Antony's treatment of her; she is surprised to learn that he has left Athens for Alexandria—and she learns that from Caesar.

It appears that Enobarbus' glowing description of Cleopatra (II. ii. 196 ff.), filling up the time while Antony is in conversation with Octavia and Caesar, is for the sake of giving information to the spectators when the play is performed. For the audience needs to have some impression of the charms of Cleopatra—and there is little of that in her actual behavior to Antony previously in the play—and the description serves as foreshadowing. And Antony's "I will to Egypt" speech, likewise foreshadowing, sounds like the momentary outburst of an exhausted man; the action it seems to determine is in no way immediate, and when it does occur is motivated, *as far as the text of the play presents it,* by cogent reasons other than, and in addition to, the magnetism of Cleopatra. But the speech is a sign that emotion, not sustained reason, will figure in the future.

If Antony is to be depicted as the hero in a tragedy, he must be shown to have some heroic qualities. That is done in the reconciliation scene, where, away from Cleopatra, he is

[12] *Shakespeare Studies* (New York, 1927), p. 111.

clear-headed, logical, controlled, stalwart. Willard Farnham is certainly right about that scene:

His meeting with Octavius and Lepidus shows him at his best as a contender for position in the world. With Octavius he takes exactly the right course, for he stands on his dignity, gives the impression of having complete confidence in the power at his command, and, though he shows defiance, makes his case in statesmanlike fashion and never lets the argument turn into a downright quarrel.[13]

It is this scene that provides the vision of what would be possible in the future if Antony would always follow reason, if he would never, as Enobarbus puts it, "make his will/Lord of his reason" (III. xiii. 3–4).[14] The scene gives the ideal, the upright, the vertical element that makes poignant in a tragedy the "How are the mighty fallen!" And so it is not only a misreading of the text and an unjustified debasing of Antony to charge him with hypocritical double-dealing in the marriage with Octavia which results from the scene; it is the destruction of an absolutely essential ingredient in the tragedy of Antony. Antony in Rome is the Antony that could become Emperor Antony, the ruler of the world.

II. ACTIUM AND AFTER

PRIOR to Actium, though Antony is in Egypt before return-ing to Rome physically and metaphorically, the stress is on Roman affairs: Antony's decision to go to Rome for the

---

[13] *Shakespeare's Tragic Frontier*, p. 176.

[14] "Will" apparently means "appetite" or "lust." See Whitaker, *Shakespeare's Use of Learning*, p. 205.

reasons given to Enobarbus with Pompey's threat as the most serious, the reconciliation with Octavius, Antony's marriage to Octavia, and Antony's proceeding to the East in management of Roman activities there. After Actium the scene is Alexandria and its environs. That transference, while historically and politically in accordance with Plutarch, is dramatically symbolic and potent, for Egypt means Cleopatra, and it marks the shift in Antony from reason to emotion as the operating factor. True it is, as noted in the previous discussion, that emotion had not been altogether absent; there were indications that emotion was not completely suppressed and they served as uncomfortable portents. The emergence of "will" as the primary force at Actium is somewhat sudden, and shocking, though there is some preparation for it in Antony's anger at the injuries he is sure Caesar has done him since leaving Rome.

Along with the hints, before Actium, of the influence of passion (in the Elizabethan sense) on Antony there should be mentioned one aspect of Antony's personality not touched on in the first section of this chapter: his liking for pleasures of the senses. That is represented in the scene on Pompey's galley (II. vii). Farnham calls it an "interlude of low comedy, . . . one of the crucial scenes . . . because of its character revelation." "Antony is thoroughly in his element, all too willing to put the cares of the world out of his mind and exercise his genius for revelry. . . . Antony dominates the revelry, but Octavius dominates the gathering." [15] To what extent his love for revelry conduces to Antony's downfall is not certain; surely it is only a part of his pleasure in Alexandria unless his love for Cleopatra is included in the idea of revelry. When in Rome he put business first, like a good

[15] Page 188.

Roman. But in a sense his love of pleasure is part of his humanity, and his concern for his soldiers, evidenced emotionally on the eve of the land skirmish (III. ii) as he shakes hands with them, praises them, bids them join with him in good cheer for the evening—with the result that even Enobarbus weeps and Cleopatra is in consternation—contrasts vividly with the coldness and lack of condescension that Caesar always shows. This scene is easily remembered later, when Caesar gives orders that the soldiers who revolted to him from Antony be put "in the van" of his army (IV. vi. 9–11).

Really of more significance than the revelry on Pompey's galley is the conversation in the preceding scene (II. vi) between Enobarbus and Menas, where the realist Enobarbus says, speaking of Antony and Caesar, and Octavia, that "the band that seems to tie their friendship together will be the very strangler of their amity" (II. vi. 128–130) and predicts that Antony "will to his Egyptian dish again" (II. vi. 134–135), and that "that which is the strength of their amity shall prove the immediate author of their variance" (II. vi. 136–138). Thus the audience is prepared for the contest between Antony and Caesar that is precipitated at Actium. But the audience is given the impression that Caesar is the initial offender, for the scene in which Antony complains to Octavia of Caesar's injuries to him (III. iv) precedes that (sc. vi) in which Caesar lists his grievances against Antony. There is no hint of a rift between Antony and Octavia before that charge by Antony of Caesar's adverse actions and violations of Antony's honor, and Antony declares to Octavia that "if I lose mine honour, / I lose myself" (III. iv. 22–23). Antony then sets about preparations for war. Caesar, like a thorough-going propagandist with a secret service ("I have eyes upon him," vi. 62), justifies himself at length to Agrippa and Maecenas (sc. vi), places all blame on Antony, emphasizes to Octavia Antony's wrongs to her (which she at first doubts), and lists in detail (III. vi. 68–76) "The kings o' th' earth" that Antony has assembled to oppose him. Thus definite and adequate warning is given of the inevitable conflict, a conflict that will decide which of the two is to be the ruler of the world.

It does come as a surprise that Antony, though opposed by Enobarbus and a representative soldier, is determined to fight at sea (III. vii. 28–49). The audience suddenly realizes how much Antony's judgment has been weakened by his stay in Egypt prior to the fight. Nor does Cleopatra show good judgment: "Cleopatra has the whim to be present in the war. Enobarbus opposes her, but he shows little respect and he treats her, not as queen of Egypt, but merely as Antony's mistress. Antony joins them. Though every reason is against it, he is for fighting at sea merely because Cleopatra so desires. Hereafter his ruin is rapid, and the effect is heightened by the speed of the episodes." [16] Reason, judgment, and honor all disappear when Antony suddenly, at the critical point in the fight, deserts the conflict and follows Cleopatra as she leaves the scene. The description of the battle (III. x. 9–21) is given "chorically in soldiers' slang, with its beast-fable metaphors to mark the fall in pitch and scale. . . . This conveys the sense of shame and humiliation of Antony only less forcibly than Antony's own outburst when at last realization comes to him." [17] Ironically Antony's vehement declaration to Octavia, "If I lose mine honour, / I lose myself," is proving to be true.

[16] G. B. Harrison, *Shakespeare's Tragedies* (London, 1951), p. 214.
[17] Griffiths, "*Antony and Cleopatra*," p. 52.

Shame and despair accompany Antony in his flight to Cleopatra's palace; there he urges his attendants to divide among them a ship laden with gold, and turn to Caesar. As for himself, "I have myself resolv'd upon a course / Which has no need of you" (III. xi. 9–10). But Cleopatra manages to obtain his pardon for her leaving the sea fight and they are reconciled.[18] There follow errors in judgment: Antony's sending of a minor person (his schoolmaster) to treat with Caesar (III. xi. 71) and the foolish challenge to Caesar to meet him in single combat (III. xii. 25–28), which disgusts Enobarbus:

> Yes, like enough high-battled Caesar will
> Unstate his happiness and be stag'd to th' show
> Against a sworder! I see men's judgments are
> A parcel of their fortunes, and things outward
> Do draw the inward quality after them
> To suffer all alike. That he should dream,
> Knowing all measures, the full Caesar will
> Answer his emptiness! Caesar, thou hast subdu'd
> His judgment too.
>
> (III. xiii. 29–37)

He begins to think about leaving Antony, wavers, but after Antony's extreme behavior in having Caesar's Thyreus whipped because he kisses Cleopatra's hand, accusing Cleo-

---

[18] See below, pp. 40–41. Griffiths comments (p. 52): "Antony is roused from [his] agony not by his own vitality or virtue but by the magnificent acting of Cleopatra, and it is the acting that we see mainly. She 'becomes' overpowering supplication and contrition: 'Pardon, pardon, pardon.' She has the eye for effect of the superb tragic actress. 'Stand by me'—she controls the whole dignified little group of suppliants of which she is the magnificently drooping central figure, inspiring them with the proper gesture and feeling of intercession—and Antony melts."

patra in his jealousy of promiscuity (ll. 116 ff.), and too readily forgiving Cleopatra after her impassioned but basically illogical plea (III. xiii. 158–167),[19] decides definitely, "I will seek / Some way to leave him" (III. xiii. 200–201).

It is through the speeches of Enobarbus that the real falling away of Antony from the upright described in the first section of this chapter is clearly, vividly depicted. Logically Enobarbus is right: if the leader proves himself utterly lacking in judgment and incompetent it is foolish to remain loyal to him: "The loyalty well held to fools doth make / Our faith mere folly" (III. xiii. 42–43). "Yet," he says,

> he that can endure
> To follow with allegiance a fall'n lord
> Does conquer him that did his master conquer
> And earns a place i' th' story.

But that was before the Thyreus scene and its consequences.

It is through the death of Enobarbus (IV. ix) that the effect on others of Antony's falling away from the upright is effectively illustrated. The dominance of passion over reason in Antony causes Enobarbus' dilemma. Reason tells him to desert Antony; his heart tells him he is wrong, and when the generous, magnanimous Antony sends to him all his treasure his heart breaks:

> I am alone the villain of the earth,
> And feel I am so most. O Antony,
> Thou mine of bounty, how wouldst thou have paid
> My better service, when my turpitude
> Thou dost so crown with gold! This blows my heart.

[19] See below, pp. 43–44.

If swift thought break it not, a swifter mean
Shall outstrike thought; but thought will do't, I feel.
I fight against thee? No! I will go seek
Some ditch wherein to die; the foul'st best fits
My latter part of life.

(IV. vi. 30–39)

And he dies with a plea to Antony for forgiveness and with
"O Antony, O Antony!" on his lips (IV. ix. 23). It is certainly not the least of Antony's mistakes that his behavior
thus causes the poignant conflict within his most loyal and
logical supporter and his eventual death. The implied contrast between Caesar and Antony is clear from the Enobarbus
episode: the lack of humanity in Caesar would have caused
Enobarbus much unhappiness; Antony's humanity, with his
weaknesses and his magnanimity, causes Enobarbus' dilemma
and pathetic consequences. Nowhere does the potential difficulty of reconciling head and heart become more clearly
depicted than in the whole relationship of Antony and
Enobarbus. The Elizabethan insistence on the necessity that
reason control passion is admirably illustrated in the failure
of Antony; Enobarbus is the innocent victim of Antony's
failure; that in a tragedy the fate of the protagonist draws
others undeservedly with it is touchingly shown by its effect
on Enobarbus. Donald A. Stauffer rightly calls Enobarbus
"a focus in which the main presented action may be scru-
tinized in miniature." [20] And his death prefigures that of
Antony.

With the voice of logic—lamentably not listened to and
heeded—forever stilled, Antony's course is soon run. The

---

[20] *Shakespeare's World of Images* (New York, 1949), p. 233.

second sea fight follows. This time Antony blames Cleopatra, not his own behavior, for his defeat:

> This foul Egyptian hath betrayed me!
>   . . . Triple-turn'd whore! 'tis thou
> Hast sold me to this novice, and my heart
> Makes only wars on thee. Bid them all fly!
> For when I am reveng'd upon my charm,
> I have done all. . . . Betray'd I am.
> O this false soul of Egypt! this grave charm—
> Whose eye beck'd forth my wars and call'd them home,
> Whose bosom was my crownet, my chief end—
> Like a right gypsy hath at fast and loose
> Beguil'd me to the very heart of loss!
> . . . The witch shall die.
>
>   (IV. xii. 10, 13-17, 24-29, 47)

When much earlier Antony declared to himself "I must from this enchanting queen break off" (I. ii. 132), the bewitching sense of "enchanting" was present. Antony did not completely "break off"; gradually and finally, after the seeming cure during his marriage to Octavia, he falls more and more inextricably into the coils of the Egyptian, and now he reiterates "charm," "gypsy," and the sense of gypsy in "Egyptian" and "Egypt." Now it is not a matter of breaking off. Heretofore Cleopatra was able to overcome his anger by impassioned pleas for pardon. Now histrionics will not serve. She calls on her women for help, and Charmian advises her to lock herself in the monument "and send him word you are dead" (IV. xiii. 4). Cleopatra, with no thought of an adverse effect on Antony, says immediately, but still with a characteristic plea for pity:

> Mardian, go tell him I have slain myself.
> Say that the last I spoke was "Antony"

And word it, prithee, piteously. Hence, Mardian,
And bring me how he takes my death.

(IV. xiii. 7–10)

In giving that order Cleopatra reveals how little she understands the Roman code; for her the idea of honor is non-existent, or grudgingly admitted as when, in I. iii, she said, "Your honour calls you hence"; but then it was *"Your* honour," not "honour." Mardian's message comes to Antony as he is condemning Cleopatra for having "Pack'd cards with Caesar and false-play'd my glory / Unto an enemy's triumph" (IV. xiv. 19–20); Mardian does word it piteously:

> Death of one person can be paid but once,
> And that she has discharg'd. What thou wouldst do
> Is done unto thy hand. The last she spake
> Was 'Antony! most noble Antony!'
> Then in the midst a tearing groan did break
> The name of Antony; it was divided
> Between her heart and lips. She rend'red life,
> Thy name so buried in her.

(IV. xiv. 27–34)

Immediately to Antony his course is clear: he will die. That Cleopatra has preceded him in honorable action as the result of his misjudging her (as he thinks) is unbearable: "I will o'ertake thee, Cleopatra, and / Weep for my pardon" (IV. xiv. 44–45):

> Eros!—I come, my queen—Eros!—Stay for me.
> Where souls do couch on flowers, we'll hand in hand
> And with our sprightly port make the ghosts gaze.
> Dido and her Æneas shall want troops,
> And all the haunt be ours.

(IV. xiv. 50–54)

To Eros, whom he has called, Antony says:

> Since Cleopatra died
> I have liv'd in such dishonour that the gods
> Detest my baseness. I . . . condemn myself to lack
> The courage of a woman—less noble mind
> Than she which by her death our Caesar tells
> 'I am conqueror of myself.'
>
> (IV. xiv. 55–62)

Nothing in the play shows more clearly the absolute difference between the Roman standards and Cleopatra's character than Antony's immediate assumption that Cleopatra killed herself through the Roman sense of honor. And nothing in the play is more pathetic than that Antony should kill himself because of Cleopatra's lie, her complete lack of the rudiments of honor being the reason for Antony's thinking that she acted—and anticipated him—according to the code. Added to that is Eros' killing himself rather than obey Antony's request, for again, Antony thinks, he has lost precedence in honor:

> Thrice nobler than myself!
> Thou teachest me, O valiant Eros, what
> I should, and thou couldst not. My queen and Eros
> Have by their brave instruction got upon me
> A nobleness in record.
>
> (IV. xiv. 95–99)

When Antony learns that Cleopatra falsified the message about her death he has no resentment; even after he is carried to Cleopatra and she pleads,

> let me rail so high
> That the false huswife Fortune break her wheel,
> Provok'd by my offence,
>
> (IV. xv. 43–45)

[31]

The Tragedies of Shakespeare's Antony and Cleopatra

he thinks of her safety and begs,

> The miserable change now at my end
> Lament nor sorrow at; but please your thoughts
> In feeding them with those my former fortunes,
> Wherein I liv'd the greatest prince o' th' world,
> The noblest; and do now not basely die,
> Not cowardly put off my helmet to
> My countryman—a Roman by a Roman
> Valiantly vanquish'd.
>
> (IV. xv. 51–58)

He is not boasting, nor does he indulge in self-pity; he touches on his "former fortunes" and his not basely dying, for the purpose of pleasing Cleopatra's thoughts and easing her sorrow, ironically in fact, for Cleopatra responds with "Noblest of men, woo't die? / Hast thou no care of me?" (IV. xv. 59–60). Though for the first time she calls him noble, she is suffused with self-pity; her failure to recognize the motives that moved Antony to kill himself is the crowning irony, and it increases greatly the pathos of Antony's tragedy.

What, then, is Antony's tragedy? It is well expressed by Enobarbus in his regret that Antony would "make his will / Lord of his reason" (III. xiii. 3–4). He possessed many virtues: courage, courtesy, generosity, liberality, magnanimity, forgiveness, the ability to think logically, firmness when at his best, humanity. But he lacked the firmness to repel the fascination of a charmer "in the East," whatever he included in the word "East." Commentators have sometimes stressed the contrast between the severity implied in "Roman" and the exoticism of the East. Perhaps that was a factor in the attraction the pleasure-loving Antony found in Cleopatra and Alexandria, though it must be remembered that Shakespeare toned down greatly the debauched Antony of Plutarch to create the Antony of his play. He was the victim of a designing charmer on one hand and of a cold, relentless, inhuman Caesar on the other. The decline is rapid after Actium, and he even gave occasional indications of self-pity, something that we never see in him before Actium. His outbursts against Cleopatra show lack of restraint, justified though they may have been; the contrast with his dignified restraint in the reconciliation scene with Caesar is a clear index to his degeneration.

Criticism of *Antony and Cleopatra,* now of tremendous volume, must be read warily, with one eye fixed on the play *as a play,* and with constant reminders that Shakespeare was writing for performance before an Elizabethan audience. Antony is presented to the audience as a man of great qualities who might have become ruler of the world but who through weaknesses made equally obvious lost the world and himself. That, the audience would perceive and understand, and that is what a sane, objective critic like M. R. Ridley understands:

A critic who sees mainly one side of Antony finds a man "of the most noble and high spirit, capable at times of a thoroughly soldier-like life, and full of kind and generous feelings." That is well said, and is true. Another, with his eyes rather on Antony's morals than his soldiership, sees that he is "dissolute and voluptuous, and Cleopatra's depravity is congenial to his nature"; that is also true, except that depravity is hardly the right word, and that it is only to one side of his nature that the "depravity" appeals. A third gives himself away by announcing that "the passion of Antony for Cleopatra is too obviously spurious to command our sympathy" (!). A fourth sees well round the subject from its various angles: "Antony appears as the soldier and the voluptuary, swayed alternately by love, by regret, by ambition, at one moment the great ruler of the divided world, at the next flinging his future away at the dictation of a passionate caprice." That I think is both justly and clearly said, and leaves little to add. Antony has a magnificent virility about him, to which both men and women react; but he is a creature of impulse, he has no eye for the stars, and cannot steer a course; he wants what he wants strongly, and he wants it immediately; he is generous, and even his faults are on a grand scale; he can descend to folly, but never to meanness.[21]

Likewise the commentary by John Munro has merit:

The tragedy was that Antony's legs, as Cleopatra put it, did indeed bestride the ocean, with one foot in Rome for awhile and the other in Alexandria. Possessed of the Roman virtues and the Roman love of indulgence, he was so caught in a snare that, called upon to exercise Roman generalship and virtues in Near Asia and Africa, he found that Egypt in the persons of Cleopatra and her folk offered more scope for luxury and indulgence than even Rome itself; until he succumbed to a thraldom which, on the one hand, exalted mere physical emotion to ennobling passion, and on the other, destroyed for ever his genius for war and government.[22]

[21] Ridley, *Antony and Cleopatra*, p. 11. An example of the fact that criticism may go to unjustifiable extremes is to be found in the following: "In the ensuing battle [Actium] he follows the Queen, even to apparent dishonour. This action must seem strange if taken on its surface meaning, but if we consider it in its inner meaning, the implication is that in the light of an eternal union the things of time become subordinate—indeed, they *must* become subordinate. It is as though we are given an image in history, which the dramatist uses, to show how human love, which is the image of God on a lower level, might in its highest form show what the love of God might be. Antony is himself, his real Self, only when he is stirred by Cleopatra." Beryl Pogson, *In the East My Pleasure Lies: an Esoteric Interpretation of Some Plays of Shakespeare* (London, 1950), p. 114.

[22] *The London Shakespeare*, VI, 1213–1214.

Antony is the opposite of Wordsworth's "happy warrior" who "through the heat of conflict, keeps the law / In calmness made, and sees what he foresaw." [23] And in every instance it is the influence of Cleopatra that lies behind the fatal mistake; but ultimately the flaw is in Antony himself: he allows his will, his passion, to become "Lord of his reason." The play presents the decline and fall of a potential Roman Emperor. But it is more than that; it is the pathetic picture of the tragic failure of a man of great virtues who by lack of consistent control over weakening tendencies, by occasional self-deception, and by love for a thoroughly unworthy object comes to a miserable end. In his tragedy, irony, manifested increasingly, becomes a most moving element, and pity—"But yet the pity of it, . . . the pity of it"—emerges and swells to become the prevailing emotional, final effect.

[23] "Character of the Happy Warrior," ll. 53–54.

◄§ III §►

Cleopatra's Tragedy

IT IS trite to remark that an audience's first impression of a character is very important; it is not commonplace to call particular attention to Cleopatra's first word in the play: "If." It is obvious—or should be—that in saying "If it be love indeed, tell me how much," she is following up a previous declaration, on Antony's part, of great love for her by teasing and bantering him. She is playful, but within her brief demand may be discerned one of her chief devices, contradiction. Immediately, by the entrance of the messenger from Rome, her tone changes; the contradictions become blunt, the taunts amazingly bold and affrontive. Antony's submitting to them proves that Philo's term "dotage" (I. i. 1) is not an exaggeration. That Cleopatra's contradictory behavior (as in I. ii. 89–91; iii. 1–5) is calculated, is obvious from her rejoinder to Charmian's warning ("In each thing give him way, cross him in nothing."): "Thou teachest like a fool. The way to lose him!" (I. iii. 10). Simultaneously Cleopatra's constant fear is revealed: that Antony will leave her.

When Antony, having determined to break off with Cleo-

patra and return to Rome, goes to her to announce his departure, she perceives that he is in a serious mood and, sur-
mising his intention, gives him no chance to talk. Six times
she interrupts him when he starts to speak. In her tirades she
taunts him (1) by references to his wife Fulvia, charging him
with falsity to her; (2) by the accusation that he has treacher-
ously betrayed her (Cleopatra); and (3) by recounting his
compliments to her when he was wooing, practically calling
him a liar. And when eventually Antony commands her to
listen to him and hear his reasons for leaving, ending with
a reference to Fulvia's death, she then accuses him of lying,
of expecting her, like a child, to believe fairy tales. When he
offers proof, the letter he has received, she then charges him
with insensibility for not weeping over his wife's death and
predicts that he would be equally unmoved by her death.
And as he protests his love for her she begins one of her
fainting spells but changes her mind; she is, she says,
"quickly ill, and well," as changeable as Antony is in his
love. She mockingly urges him to produce some tears for
Fulvia and pretend they are for her, ridicules him for not
making a better show at weeping, and calls on Charmian to
join her in laughing at Antony's rising anger.

Antony turns to walk away. Then Cleopatra brings him
back by the one appeal that just then could do it, a quavering
"Courteous lord." It is the first time in the play that she
has spoken to him in anything like a complimentary fashion.
Then she pretends to have something serious to say, or that
she was going to say but has now forgot. Antony recognizes
that she is playing for time, and she perceives his recognition.[1] She has drawn on her coquette's kit for a variety of

---

[1] Some critics have interpreted the "Courteous lord" speech differ-
ently; e.g., H. N. Hillebrand, *Antony and Cleopatra,* "The Arden

tools, and they have failed her, even her appeal to pity (her most effective, much used tool); Antony is going despite all she can do. But perhaps, if she says something kind for once, it may eventually bring him back:

> Your honour calls you hence;
> Therefore be deaf to my unpitied folly,
> And all the gods go with you! Upon your sword
> Sit laurel victory, and smooth success
> Be strew'd before your feet!

$$\text{(I. iii. 97–101)}$$

Or something that may seem kind! Her reference to his honor is much belated; she makes another appeal to pity; and the sequence of *s* sounds and the concatenation of *b*'s and *f*'s and *e*'s and *t*'s in the last line may suggest, by the conceivable hissing and sneering, an unconscious extrusion of her essentially serpentine nature.

During Antony's absence Cleopatra's behavior is self-characterizing. She evinces no interest in the business he is engaged in; she is concerned as to what he may be thinking of her, is enveloped in thoughts physical and sensual, and reviews the list of her great lovers, "Broad-fronted Caesar," "great Pompey," "brave Mark Antony." She revels in memories of her behavior to Antony—trickery in fishing, laughing him out of and into patience, dressing him in tires and mantles while she "wore his sword Philippan," contrarieties

---

Shakespeare" (Boston, 1926), p. 145: "Until now Cleopatra has been desperately trying, with all the battery of her wit and sarcasm, to stave off the moment of parting. When at last she sees that Antony is inflexible, that he is in fact on the point of strategic flight, she suddenly breaks, abandons her attack, and becomes wholly the unhappy, loving woman." But she does not "abandon her attack"; she merely changes tactics.

all. She is aghast when the news comes that Antony has married Octavia and beats the messenger, but regains hope from the description he gives of her.

We do not see Antony and Cleopatra together again until just before the battle of Actium. Were it not for Enobarbus' description of her on the river Cydnus and his analysis of her charms (II. ii. 195–245), there would be little about her in the first half of the play that to an objective reader is alluring. But even Enobarbus' account hints at Cleopatra's oppositeness, for he pictures Antony, "Enthron'd i' th' market place," waiting for Cleopatra to appear before him, which she does not do, and accepting her refusal to dine with him and her counterinvitation "to come and suppe with her." [2] The description follows closely the reconciliation scene between Antony and Octavius in which Antony, then at his best, is shown as firm master of himself and thus provides the background to contrast with his sorry self when manipulated by Cleopatra. But there is no such admirable background for Cleopatra; it is apparent that her tragedy will have to be of a distinctly different sort from Antony's. It cannot be a "tragic fall," for there is nothing for her to fall from.

[2] North's Plutarch: "*Antonius* . . . sent to command *Cleopatra* to appeare personally before him, when he came into CILICIA, to aunswere vnto such accusations as were laide against her, being this: that she had aided *Cassius* and *Brutus* in their warre against him. . . . Therefore when she was sent vnto by diuers letters, both from *Antonius* himselfe, and also from his friendes, she made so light of it and mocked *Antonius* so much, that she disdained to set forward otherwise, but to take her barge in the riuer of Cydnus. . . . When *Cleopatra* landed, *Antonius* sent to inuite her to supper to him. But she sent him worde againe, he should doe better rather to come and suppe with her."

After Actium, where Antony at her urging has fought at sea, she offers as her reason for leaving the scene of the battle that she was afraid. But that reason does not satisfy everyone. Stoll, for instance, lists among various unanswered questions in Shakespeare's plays the query "Why does Cleopatra flee from battle and Antony?"[3] Later he wonders whether in examining such a question as that, and about her later dealings with Thyreus and her responsibility in the second sea fight, we may not be "then considering too curiously."[4] Certainly the question about her behavior at Actium exists and must be considered; but just as certainly it cannot be answered.[5] Cleopatra's "I little thought / You would have followed" (III. xi. 55–56), besides putting the blame on him, may reveal a more nearly true reason than her "fearful sails": Is her leaving the battle at the critical point a test of Antony, to see whether the political leader or the lover is stronger in him? Does she fear that military success and political mastery would be a dangerous rival to her charms? And when Antony reproaches her with

> You did know
> How much you were my conqueror, and that
> My sword, made weak by my affection, would
> Obey it on all cause
>
> (III. xi. 65–68)

[3] *Shakespeare Studies,* p. 29.
[4] *Poets and Playwrights* (Minneapolis, 1930), p. 2.
[5] Enobarbus, in saying to Cleopatra,

> What though you fled
> From that great face of war whose several ranges
> Frighted each other?
>
> (III. xiii. 4–6)

is not concerned with arguing about her reason for leaving; he is condemning Antony for having followed her (ll. 6–12).

and she cries "Pardon, pardon!" is she really sorry? Her behavior to Thyreus soon after makes us wonder.

When Thyreus tells Cleopatra that

> He [Caesar] knows that you embrace not Antony
> As you did love, but as you fear'd him
>
> (III. xiii. 56–57)

she exclaims "O!" What does she mean by that? There are those who seem to know; e.g., G. L. Kittredge (note on l. 57): "Cleopatra's exclamation is meant to convey to Thyreus not only eager acceptance of Caesar's theory of her union with Antony, but also gratified surprise that Caesar should have shown so sympathetic an understanding of the case. All this she expresses in plain terms in her next speech: 'He is a god,' etc." That interpretation implies that Cleopatra, suddenly perceiving a way out of the impasse, is deserting Antony and preparing to entangle Caesar in her "toils of grace," through the pity for her that she hopes to inspire. But conceivably the "O!" may merely imply painful shock at the idea that anyone could even think she feared Antony and did not love him.[6] If so, the idea of appealing to Caesar's pity may not occur at the moment but be suggested by Thyreus'

> The scars upon your honour, therefore, he
> Does pity, as constrained blemishes,
> Not as deserv'd.
>
> (III. xiii. 58–60)

It is doubtful whether one is justified in saying "All this she expresses in plain terms in her next speech," inasmuch as

---

[6] The Folio "Oh" followed by a period may suggest only a distressful moan; Thyreus goes on speaking as if he heard nothing.

Thyreus' statement comes between her "O!" and "her next speech." Or, perhaps, the previous lines should be taken into consideration; Thyreus says,

> Caesar entreats
> Not to consider in what case thou stand'st
> Further than he is Caesar,
>
> (III. xiii. 53-55)

which seems, to her, at least, to promise noble treatment, with possible emphasis on the good will of Caesar the man. If the idea of attempting to entangle Caesar has already occurred to her, her enthusiastic "Go on. Right royal!" is flattery intended to be relayed to Caesar. But then Thyreus'

> He knows that you embrace not Antony
> As you did love, but as you fear'd him

is definitely cooling, and her "O!" may involuntarily escape her, indicating sudden awareness of Caesar's idea that she "embraced" Antony because of his power more than for love of the man himself and thus is on guard against any designs she might have on him now that he has conquered Antony. If that is the situation, then Thyreus' speech suggesting Caesar's pity for the scars upon her honor "as constrained blemishes, / Not as deserv'd" arouses hope and prompts her flattering and pity-inviting

> He is a god, and knows
> What is most right. Mine honour was not yielded
> But conquer'd merely,
>
> (III. xi. 60-62)

a bare-faced lie, as Enobarbus recognizes.

Whatever the significance of the "O!" it is soon obvious

that Cleopatra proceeds to cajole Thyreus,[7] hoping thereby to make him a friend in court. But whether she is actually deserting Antony and staking all on a hope of ensnaring Caesar or is planning a deep deception of Caesar it is impossible to tell. Nor is her behavior to Antony clear when he enters unexpectedly and in fury orders punishment to Thyreus and condemns her. She attempts to defend herself with four questions: "O, is't come to this?" "Wherefore is this?" "Have you done yet?" and, after a parenthetical "I must stay his time," "Not know me yet?" What does she mean by the fourth question? She probably intends for Antony to understand that she was just temporizing, meeting Caesar's suspected treachery with pretended submission. When Antony, still pained by what he is sure is betrayal of him, asks, "Cold-hearted toward me?" she breaks out in impassioned speech:

> Ah, dear, if I be so,
> From my cold heart let heaven engender hail,
> And poison it in the source, and the first stone
> Drop in my neck; as it determines, so
> Dissolve my life! The next Caesarion smite!
> Till by degrees the memory of my womb
> Together with my brave Egyptians all,
> By the discandying of this pelleted storm,
> Lie graveless, till the flies and gnats of Nile
> Have buried them for prey!
>
> (III. xiii. 158–167)

Actually her plea that, if her heart is cold, from it hail, poisoned in its source (her heart), should be "engendered"

[7] "And she gives Thyreus her hand to kiss. Perhaps she finds him rather good-looking; certainly she is musing on former, or on future, conquests." Speaight, *Nature in Shakespearian Tragedy*, p. 142.

only to fall in her neck, melt, and in melting dissolve her life, is basically nonsense. For if there were enough poison in the source, her heart, to kill her when, incorporated into hail, it was carried to her neck and then caused her life to dissolve, she would have been dead long ago. To say nothing of the amount of poison it would take to dispose of Caesarion and "my brave Egyptians all"! She has created a barrage of words that by the excess of emotion and the deficiency of sense seem to denote complete devotion to Antony but which by the very excesses suggest the opposite. "The lady doth protest too much, methinks." Her speech is not the bald lie that she tells Antony later when she sends him word that she has killed herself, but there is possible deception, masked by the barrage of words and the vehemence of her utterance.[8]

What a narrow escape that was for her! She has convinced Antony but not Enobarbus. For when Antony forgives her ("I am satisfied"), declares that he will fight Caesar again, calls for his captains to join him in "one other gaudy night," and boasts,

> The next time I do fight,
> I'll make Death love me; for I will contend
> Even with his pestilent scythe,
>
> (III. xiii. 192–194)

Enobarbus says, in soliloquy:

> Now he'll outstare the lightning. To be furious
> Is to be frighted out of fear, and in that mood

---

[8] Harrison, *Shakespeare's Tragedies,* p. 218, calls that speech "the first outburst of genuine emotion that she has yet shown," and adds, "It is difficult to know at this point whether Cleopatra is loyal or false; probably she does not know herself."

The dove will peck the estridge. I see still
A diminution in our captain's brain
Restores his heart. When valour preys on reason,
It eats the sword it fights with.

(III. xiii. 195–200)

Though Enobarbus speaks only of Antony, he reveals his interpretation of Cleopatra's behavior in the crisis.

The next morning Cleopatra playfully helps Antony don his armor and kisses him as he departs for battle. She comments to Charmian, "He goes forth gallantly," and expresses a wish

That he and Caesar might
Determine this great war in single fight!
Then Antony—but now—

(IV. iv. 36–38)

Since she apparently thinks Antony will be defeated, she is surprised at his victorious return:

Lord of lords!
O infinite virtue, com'st thou smiling from
The world's great snare [9] uncaught?

(IV. viii. 16–18)

Though she thus compliments Antony in exaggerated terms and promises Scarus an extravagant reward ("An armour all of gold"), she hardly discloses her real thoughts. Nor is it certain that she did not betray Antony in the second sea fight. Antony is sure: "This foul Egyptian hath betrayed

[9] Does she mean war, or "all the snares the world can set" (Ridley), or Caesar?

me!" (IV. xii. 10) and he is exceedingly bitter about the "triple-turn'd whore" that

> Like a right gypsy hath at fast and loose
> Beguil'd me to the very heart of loss!

He calls for Eros, but Cleopatra appears, having mistakenly thought, perhaps, that Antony was summoning her by calling on the deity of love, Eros—it would never occur to her that Antony was calling for Eros to have him fulfill his promise to kill Antony if Antony's code of honor should demand—and is met by "Ah, thou spell! Avaunt!" In innocence or seeming innocence she asks, "Why is my lord enrag'd against his love?" Then at Antony's threats she leaves. Exclaiming that he is "more mad / Than Telamon for his shield" (xiii. 1–2) she sends Mardian to Antony:

> Mardian, go tell him I have slain myself.
> Say that the last I spoke was 'Antony'
> And word it, prithee, piteously. Hence, Mardian,
> And bring me how he takes my death.[10]
>
> (IV. xiii. 7–10)

The lie, with the appeals for pity, is her final deception of Antony. Knowledge about how he takes her death may be intended to provide her with a clue as to possible appeasement of his wrath, but the lie is the climax of all her tricks, and ironically spurs Antony on to kill himself. Though it be argued that she did not betray Antony, his thinking she did is understandable, in the light of her behavior throughout the play up to the time of the second sea fight.

---

[10] The irony at this point is unmistakable and exquisite. Cleopatra's ignorance of the Roman code that demands that the hopelessly defeated general commit suicide, though here indirectly by the sword of Eros, is matched by her lie that she committed suicide for love of Antony.

What would be—to return to Cleopatra's entrance and exit for a moment—the impression on an audience of Cleopatra's behavior? Antony's brief but vivid description of the fleet's surrender and his repeated charge that Cleopatra has betrayed him, plus remembrance of what happened at Actium, may well make an audience suspicious of her when she appears. And her exit, following upon Antony's detailed picture of her as the captive of Caesar and the victim of Octavia's wrath, may well give the definite impression that her self-interest has been and is the force that motivates her action. She does not even think of fainting or of attempting to kill herself in disproof of Antony's accusation. And her question "Why is my lord enrag'd against his love?" is colored by her accustomed plea for pity. Altogether, whether or not she betrayed Antony to Caesar is left an unanswered question, like the motives for her behavior at Actium.

There are some obvious facts. Cleopatra, to satisfy her ego, must have as her lovers the world's greatest. The outcome of the war between Antony and Caesar, since it is for world mastery, will determine which will emerge as the greater. Suppose Antony should win: he will certainly be immersed in state affairs and neglect her. Suppose Caesar should win: then there is the question as to whether she can ensnare him. Her equivocal behavior to Antony and her flirting with Caesar through Thyreus may reflect her uncertainty.

Yet there can be no doubt that Cleopatra has love, of a sort, for Antony, and when he, dying, is brought to her in the monument it is the realization of his personality as a man, her lover, and her belated recognition of the stalwart Roman qualities he represents (emphasized, for her comfort, in his dying speech) that for the moment overshadow everything else. Even though self-pity is not completely absent—

"Noblest of men, woo't die? / Hast thou no care of me?"
(IV. xv. 59–60)—she is genuine in lamenting that "The
crown o' th' earth doth melt," and she is quite humbled:

> No more but e'en a woman, and commanded
> By such poor passion as the maid that milks
> And does the meanest chares.
>
> (IV. xv. 73–75)

Some appreciation of Antony's worth, now that he is no
more, comes to her:

> It were for me
> To throw my sceptre at the injurious gods,
> To tell them that this world did equal theirs
> Till they had stol'n our jewel.
>
> (IV. xv. 75–78)

But there is no admitting, apparently no perception, of the
fact that she is responsible for his defeat and death. Her
self-pity, her concentration on self, makes it impossible for
her to see the situation objectively. If she could see it objectively, she would not be Cleopatra. It is her very Cleopatra-
ness that is the basis for her ultimate tragedy. If she were
a Juliet she would kill herself immediately for love of
Antony, not merely talk about suicide. The fact that she
does not act, but talks, precludes any interpretation of her
tragedy as a love tragedy, even though there is pathos in

> what's brave, what's noble,
> Let's do it after the high Roman fashion
> And make death proud to take us.
>
> (IV. xv. 86–88)

She has learned something; she has gained unconsciously
some insight into what virtue, Roman virtue as embodied

in Antony, is. There is no sneering now at "a Roman thought" (I. ii. 87). But though she knows no "friend / But resolution and the briefest end," she is yet a long way from declaring "Husband, I come"; her tragedy is by no means yet manifest.

When we next see her (V. ii) some time has elapsed; she still talks of suicide, but not of "the briefest end": "My desolation does begin to make / A better life." Better than what? Since she immediately speaks of Caesar and his subjection to Fortune, she will show a "life" superior to his by doing that which ends all the influence of Fortune. Is it unconscious irony that she uses the word "life" in speaking of the ending of her life? Her whole speech (ll. 1–8) is of herself in relation to Caesar, and she does not attempt suicide until the Roman guardsmen make a move to capture her. Meanwhile she has parleyed with Proculeius and through him made a bid for pity from Caesar—"a queen his beggar" —and professes "A doctrine of obedience." But she adds, significantly, "and would gladly / Look him i' th' face" (ll. 31–32).

When she is prevented from killing herself (not for love of Antony but to forestall capture) she moans,

> Where art thou, death?
> Come hither, come! Come, come, and take a queen
> Worth many babes and beggars.
>
> (V. ii. 46–48)

The real reason for her attempted suicide is made plain by her outburst after Proculeius' "O, temperance, lady!":

> Sir, I will eat no meat; I'll not drink, sir;
> If idle talk will once be necessary,
> I'll not sleep neither. This mortal house I'll ruin,

Do Caesar what he can. Know, sir, that I
Will not wait pinion'd at your master's court
Nor once be chastis'd with the sober eye
Of dull Octavia. Shall they hoist me up
And show me to the shouting varletry
Of censuring Rome? Rather a ditch in Egypt
Be gentle grave unto me! Rather on Nilus' mud
Lay me stark-nak'd and let the waterflies
Blow me into abhorring! Rather make
My country's high pyramides my gibbet
And hang me up in chains!

(V. ii. 49–62)

Proculeius had been commended to her by Antony (IV. xv. 47–48), but he has proved untrustworthy. When Dolabella follows and attempts to gain her confidence by "Most noble Empress, you have heard of me?" (V. ii. 71), she tests him: "You laugh when boys or women tell their dreams; / Is't not your trick?" He does not understand what she means, and is puzzled as she pours out an elaborate eulogy of Antony (V. ii. 79 ff.). She glorifies Antony's power and bounty and wins Dolabella's sympathy to the degree that he answers truthfully her question as to what Caesar intends to do with her: lead her in triumph in Rome.[11] She has told Dolabella that she "dreamt there was an Emperor Antony" and asked whether "there was or might be such a man / As this I dreamt of." It appears that she was giving him an opportunity to assure her that Caesar, now Emperor, is such a man;[12]

[11] Farnham asks (*Shakespeare's Tragic Frontier*, p. 198): "Why . . . should she be worried about what Caesar means to do with her if she has fully made up her mind to leave the dull world that no longer contains Antony?"

[12] This Dolabella incident has been interpreted in various ways. For instance, Griffiths, *"Antony and Cleopatra,"* p. 64: "Cleopatra

since he did not respond affirmatively, she puts her direct question. Immediately after his answer, Caesar enters.

It is through the glorified Antony of her dream that the audience is made aware of the fact that Cleopatra now has gained some conception of the worth of Antony. But that is in retrospect; she indicated no such recognition while Antony was alive. The idealization of Antony in the dream contrasts with the unideal realism of her treatment of him while he lived. (Dramatically, the idealized Antony comes between the deceitful Proculeius and the cold, unmalleable Caesar. Cleopatra's acquired recognition of Antony's excellence cannot be left to the very end of the play but must be made evident, for it is vital to the formation of her tragedy.) But she is in many ways still the former Cleopatra; she schemes, and uses a new device to arouse pity for herself. There is no admission of responsibility for what has happened, no hint of a sense of guilt. And she obviously has not given up hope of a future if one can be contrived that is not shameful to her. That future depends on what she can gain from Caesar.

turns this great engine of poetry on Dolabella, but it remains primarily an apology for suicide and a declaration of faith in a love, a person that has been and is no more in time." For another:

This high-sounding praise of her last lover is wholly genuine. . . . But Cleopatra is an infinite coquette . . . she has never been able to 'see an ambassador, scarcely even a messenger, without desiring to bewitch him'; and only death can put an end to her instinctive longing to fascinate men . . . Cleopatra is eloquent both because she is praising her beloved Antony, and because she is captivating Dolabella. Her rapturous words are about Antony, but they are also directed at her new admirer. . . . Dolabella . . . returns to declare his love, to give the queen the fullest possible information, and to take a last farewell.

Most students of Shakespeare do not seem to realize the full force of this embryonic love-affair, acting itself out before us on the very brink of the grave. [A. H. Tolman, *Act V of "Antony and Cleopatra," Falstaff and Other Shakespearean Topics* (New York, 1925), pp. 166–167.]

Since she is still alive and has not become penitent nor admitted—even realized—any responsibility for the dire situation she is now in, it is inevitable that she should carry on. Indeed the force of momentum, not checked by a change in character, leads the audience to anticipate an attempt to captivate Caesar: Julius Caesar, Pompey, Antony; and now Octavius is Caesar, the world's greatest.[13] And it is to be expected that she will use the old tools, or rather the most effective one, the appeal to pity.[14] When Caesar enters, she kneels to him:

> Sir, the gods
> Will have it thus. My master and my lord
> I must obey;
>
> (V. ii. 115–117)

then

> Sole sir o' th' world,
> I cannot project mine own cause so well
> To make it clear; but do confess I have
> Been laden with like frailties which before
> Have often sham'd our sex.
>
> (V. ii. 120–124)

[13] "Each person [in a story or play] must behave in character; that means that he must do what from their [the readers'] knowledge of him they expect him to do." Somerset Maugham, *The Summing Up*, Chap. 72.

[14] The sequence of seeing, pitying, and loving is explicitly stated, though by a woman for a man in this instance, in *The Two Noble Kinsmen*, II. iv. 7, 11, 14–15:

> *Daughter.* First, I saw him;
> . . . next I pitied him;
> . . . then I loved him,
> Extremely lov'd him, infinitely lov'd him.

Caesar's response gives her little encouragement, ending as it does with a threat:

> If you apply yourself to our intents,
> Which towards you are most gentle, you shall find
> A benefit in this change; but, if you seek
> To lay on me a cruelty by taking
> Antony's course, you shall bereave yourself
> Of my good purposes, and put your children
> To that destruction which I'll guard them from
> If thereon you rely.
>
> (V. ii. 126-133)

There follows the Seleucus incident. Whether she is providing for herself if she should have a future or, as some think, trying to convince Caesar by the planned exposure of her concealing half her wealth that she has no intention of following "Antony's course," or has contrived the whole thing as a means of eliciting pity, she unquestionably utilizes it for the latter purpose:

> O Caesar, what a wounding shame is this,
> That thou vouchsafing here to visit me,
> Doing the honour of thy lordliness
> To one so meek, that mine own servant should
> Parcel the sum of my disgraces by
> Addition of his envy! Say, good Caesar,
> That I some lady trifles have reserv'd,
> Immoment toys, things of such dignity
> As we greet modern friends withal; and say
> Some nobler token I have kept apart
> For Livia and Octavia—must I be unfolded
> With one that I have bred? The gods! It smites me
> Beneath the fall I have. . . .
> Be it known that we, the greatest, are misthought
> For things that others do; and, when we fall,

We answer others' merits in our name,
Are therefore to be pitied.

(V. ii. 159–179)

But her flattery, her profession of complete subjection to him, and her tearful appeals for pity have no effect on the astute Caesar, who answers her by the royal "we" and to her final, more quaveringly piteous "My master and my lord," says bluntly, "Not so. Adieu." She has done her best, but her practised methods, particularly the previously much-used pleas for pity, do not touch Caesar. And when he leaves she is vehement in her outburst—"He words me, girls, he words me," and adds "that I should not / Be noble to myself!" [15] There is nothing left for her but to fall back on her resolution. The confirmation by Dolabella of what he had already told her about Caesar's intentions and his specification of a time limit,

Caesar through Syria
Intends his journey, and within three days
You with your children will he send before,

(V. ii. 200–202)

incites her to immediate action. She describes vividly to Iras the exhibition Caesar would make in Rome of Iras and herself (she would no doubt include Charmian if she were then present) and applauds Iras' determination to pluck out her eyes rather than see it—

Why, that's the way
To fool their preparation and to conquer
Their most absurd intents.

(V. ii. 224–226)

---

[15] Apparently "a desire to save herself from the ignoble fate that Caesar plans for her." Farnham, *Shakespeare's Tragic Frontier*, p. 199. But is that really all she means?

Caesar having proved to be untouched, she reverts to the scene of her conquest of Antony:

> Show me, my women, like a queen. Go fetch
> My best attires. I am again for Cydnus,
> To meet Mark Antony.
>
> (V. ii. 227–229)

With an implied confession of dillydallying, she declares:

> My resolution's plac'd, and I have nothing
> Of woman in me. Now from head to foot
> I am marble-constant. Now the fleeting moon
> No planet is of mine.
>
> (V. ii. 238–241)

In her final moments, as she carries out her resolution, Cleopatra has "immortal longings," hears Antony call, gloats over outwitting Caesar, addresses Antony as "husband," shows jealousy in her fear that Iras may gain the first other-world kiss from Antony, sneers at Caesar again, speaks lovingly to the asp at her breast,[16] and dies with "Antony" on her lips and with a final fling of contempt for the world. But, it should be noted, she does not "do it after the high Roman fashion," nor with the singleness of motive that actuated Antony, whose tragedy gains ironical poignancy because he thought Cleopatra—really the lying Cleopatra—had anticipated him in nobility (IV. xiv. 55–62).

Does she kill herself to be with Antony or to escape Caesar? It is the final question, to be placed along with others. Would

---

[16] "The asp, wriggling its way from the basket to her breast, carries more than its mortal sting; it bears the salt and savour of all that natural life whose passionate child Cleopatra had been. The asp is very much more than a theatrical convenience; it is the symbol of nature reclaiming one part of its own." Speaight, *Nature in Shakespearian Tragedy*, p. 139.

she have killed herself if she could have added Caesar to her string of "greats"? Why did she leave the battle of Actium? Why did she urge Antony to fight at sea? Did she betray Antony in the second sea fight? What was the meaning of her "O!"? Why did she behave in such a way as to lose her country instead of preserve it? Did she ever really love Antony or did she love herself for having captivated him? Why did she tease, taunt, and cross Antony, very rarely saying anything kind to him? These questions, and others that could be asked, show that it was not accidental that the first word she speaks in the play is "If." The appropriate symbol for her is a big interrogation point.

There is testimony, of course, by Antony and especially by Enobarbus, the clear-headed, cynical logician, as to her infinite variety. Somehow she has enchanted the world's greatest men, and she is beloved by her attendants, even to the death. But in her behavior throughout the play, from the effrontery of her appearing on the Cydnus to her wily proceedings with Octavius Caesar, there are repeated evidences that she is unaccountable. It is certain that Antony never penetrates her real character; he may call her gypsy and witch, but that is begging the question. How, in the face of and through his presentation of Cleopatra's behavior to Antony, does Shakespeare make of her a force powerful enough to bring about the downfall of the great Antony? Does he not supply the answer, paradoxically, by depicting her as alluring and magnetic because of all the unanswerable questions about her? Does he not imply that the secret of her charm lies in the fact that neither Antony nor we (including Shakespeare himself) can identify the secret of her charm? Such an interpretation was suggested by Gamaliel Bradford many years ago but apparently disregarded by most commentators on the play:

> I have said that Cleopatra was mysterious. Perhaps it is an element of the art of Shakespeare to puzzle us a little, to make us feel that we cannot interpret him always conclusively. It detracts nothing from the truth of his characters that we cannot always determine what their motives are as we can with that poor little creature of Dryden. . . . I, at least, do not feel clear as to her good faith to Antony. That she loves him there is no doubt at all, loves him as she is capable of loving. But it is more than doubtful whether she kills herself for love of him or in sheer desperation to avoid the scorn and vengeance of Caesar. I greatly fear that if she had been confident of Caesar's favor, confident of reigning in Rome as she had reigned in Alexandria, Antony's poor dust might have tossed forgotten in the burning winds of Egypt. And yet, I do not know—who can know? That is precisely what gives the character its charm.[17]

But whatever interpretation of Cleopatra's character may be given—and to survey all that has been said would demand a volume devoted to her—the final question remains: What is *her tragedy?* One can agree with Farnham's statement that "It is part of her tragedy that with her subtlety she wins control of his [Antony's] force and by winning this control ruins him and herself,"[18] but that is by no means the whole story. Nor is it satisfactory to become rhapsodic, to glorify Cleopatra beyond warrant, as J. Middleton Murry does:

> Now [after Antony's death] in very deed, Cleopatra loves Antony: now she discerns his royalty, and loyalty surges up in her to meet it. Now we feel that her wrangling with Caesar and her Treasurer which follows is all external to her—as it were a

---

[17] "The Serpent of Old Nile," *Poet Lore*, X (1898), 529–530.
[18] Farnham, p. 174.

part which she is still condemned to play 'in this vile world':
a mere interruption, an alien interlude, while the travail of
fusion between the order of imagination and love, and the order
of existence and act is being accomplished: till the flame of perfect purpose breaks forth [V. ii. 226–229 quoted]. No, not *again*
for Cydnus: but now for the first time, indeed. For that old
Cydnus, where the wonder pageant was, was but a symbol and
prefiguration of this. That was an event in time; this is an
event in eternity. And those royal robes were then only lovely
garments of the body, now they are the integument of a soul.
They must show her like a queen, now, because she *is* a queen,
as she never was before.[19]

Much nearer to the text of the play and to all the evidence is
Stoll:

. . . in [an] . . . audacious, sensuous key, for all her exaltation,
she expresses herself on her deathbed. She is tenderer with her
women, and stronger and more constant, than she has ever been;
but her thoughts of Antony, though now an inviolable shade,
are not celestial or Platonic. They are steeped in amorousness,
and she is waiting, coiled on her couch. She loves him more
than at the beginning; but neither now nor at his death is she,
as Professor Schücking declares, "all tenderness, all passionate
devotion and unselfish love"; nor does she quit life because it is
not worth the living. On life she really never loosens her greedy
grip. Her beauty she clutches to her dying bosom as the miser
does his gold. Her robe and jewels are, even in death, assumed
to heighten the impression of it upon Caesar—though only to
show him what he has missed. She hears Antony mock him now,
from over the bitter wave; and at the beginning of the scene
she cried,

> go fetch
> My best attires; I am again for Cydnus—

as one who, to please him and herself, and vex their rival,
would fain die at her best, reviving all the glories of that triumph.

[19] *Shakespeare,* pp. 375–376.

To an ugly death she could scarcely have brought herself;. . . the death which . . . she is choosing and devising [is] . . . an event, a scene, well-nigh an amour . . . she thinks the stroke of death is as a lover's pinch, which hurts and is desired. . . . she is wrapped and folded up in sensuous imaginations to the end.[20]

Indeed, to have Cleopatra glorified and transfigured is to forgive her treatment of Antony, to imply that it was well worth the destruction of the great Roman to bring about her regeneration. If the tragedy of Antony and the tragedy of Cleopatra are to interact to intensify each other, as they do, it is necessary *not* to have a transfiguration of Cleopatra; the poignancy of Antony's tragedy is intensified by Cleopatra's unregeneracy, and it increases the pathos and tragedy of Cleopatra that she is never penitent, not even conscious of the debacle she has wrought. That she does change some-what, that she does attain some realization of what Antony was, is to be recognized. That she did not realize it earlier, and to a much greater degree, is her tragedy: the too little and the too late. Thus the tragedy of Cleopatra is different in kind from that of Antony; the play contains the tragedy of Antony and then the tragedy of Cleopatra.

The "too little" involves a considerable pathetic element. Cleopatra, though appearing on the Cydnus as Venus, is really Isis in environment, interests, and obsessions. Of that the fertility connotations made obvious in the conversation of her companions Iras and Charmian with the Soothsayer (I. ii), the Nile imagery frequent in the play, and the trend of Cleopatra's own thoughts as revealed in her speeches give plentiful proof. Her basic interests show themselves in her imagination as she visualizes Antony in Rome (I. v. 19 ff.). They permeate the glowing dream of Antony she describes to Dolabella, as she concentrates on Antony's power and his

[20] *Poets and Playwrights,* pp. 14–16.

bounty (not on aspects of character and personal qualities). They suffuse her final speeches; "but even then what emerges is a state of trance, a vision of the divine lover Antony, filling Heaven and Earth, the kiss of the bridegroom, Love lifted to a higher plane among the Homeric gods, all an aspiration and a wild desire, the eagle and the dove." [21] This last characterization of her vision is over-etherealized; a more moderate statement is Farnham's (p. 202):

> If we are to understand that the love of Cleopatra for Antony, like her character, continues to be deeply flawed to the end of her life, we are nevertheless to understand that, like her character, it has its measure of nobility. If Cleopatra never comes to have a love for Antony to match his love for her, she at least comes to have magnificent visions of what it would be like to achieve such a love, and her climactic vision leads her to call him husband as she dies.

To that extent we may credit Cleopatra with some ennobling; but it is just enough to intensify and illuminate her tragedy. "She's good, being gone; / The hand could pluck her back that shov'd her on," said Antony (I. ii. 130–131), on hearing of Fulvia's death. Cleopatra only after Antony's death comes to some realization of what he was; he's good, being gone. Only after he is wounded or dead does she call him "noble"; only in a sort of funeral hymn does she recognize his power and bounty. But she never feels any sense of guilt such as Antony confesses; there is no *peccavi;* there is no repentance, no consciousness even, of the need for remorse. She is no Othello; her tragedy can be only partial, not complete.

Cleopatra's tragedy is inherent in her equivocality, in her utter self-interest, and in her complete ignorance of the existence of an unselfish love apart from the physical. She has

[21] Griffiths, *"Antony and Cleopatra,"* p. 42.

had no comprehension of Roman virtues, no recognition of Antony's fundamental character, no appreciation of his courtesy and devotion to her. She gloried in his greatness as a soldier and as the most powerful of the Triumvirs, not for his sake but for her own—and undermined both his military prowess and his power. She evinces, throughout the play, little concern about the country of which she is queen; she is woman, not queen, in her interests and behavior. She is as innocent of morality as Falstaff of honor. But she does learn something, through frustration and suffering, of what virtue —Roman virtue—means. It is pathetic and tragic that a beginning of anything other than sensual self-interest comes when there is neither the opportunity nor the time for growth to ensue. In that irony—in the too little and the too late— lies her tragedy. That is all the tragedy there is for her, but it is none the less profound, and gains poignancy through contrast to Antony's as his gains pathos through contrast to hers.

A Note on Enobarbus

THE IRONY in Enobarbus' bold remarks to Antony (I. ii. 137–182) is not always perceived. For example, Griffiths, *"Antony and Cleopatra,"* p. 39, states that "Enobarbus does not think of her [Cleopatra] as a 'person' or a 'character' at all, she is a phenomenon, 'a wonderful piece of work'" and "he describes her passions as 'made of nothing but the finest parts of pure love.'" He accepts Enobarbus' statements at face value, not perceiving that he is bantering Antony; his contradictions, his punning, his exaggerations, his boldness and bluntness are his method of trying to turn Antony against Cleopatra and send him back to Rome and the main chance. Likewise Daniel Stempel, in "The Transmigration of the Crocodile," *Shakespeare Quarterly,* VII (1956), avers that "In the earlier scenes Enobarbus makes no attempt to recall Antony to reason" (p. 66) and that "he does not rebuke Antony for his attachment to Cleopatra" (p. 65). He cannot, of course, "rebuke" his superior officer, but he can—and does—use irony to the same purpose.

More to the point is the comment by E. C. Wilson, in "Shakespeare's Enobarbus," *Joseph Quincy Adams: Memorial Studies* (Washington, 1948), pp. 392–393:

Antony, sobered by news of Fulvia's death, declares that he must from "this enchanting queen break off." Enobarbus banteringly cries, "Why, then we kill all our women. We see how mortal an unkindness is to them. If they suffer our departure, death's the word." But in his next speech, a reply to Antony's "I must be gone," his clear sense of Antony's folly pierces through his banter: "Under a compelling occasion, let women die. It were pity to cast them away for nothing, though, between them and a great cause they should be esteemed nothing." Nowhere in the play is there a more incisive judgment on Antony's conduct. Mockingly Enobarbus salutes the "wonderful piece of work" that holds his master in thrall; yet comprehension of Cleopatra's spell is within his irony—"Her passions are made of nothing but the finest part of pure love." Enobarbus is too alive to the humor of the situation not to continue in his *goguenard* vein until Antony, wincing, commands that his "light answers" cease.

One may question the "humor of the situation" idea; it may be pretended humor, but Enobarbus is too serious in his purpose to talk idly. Actually for Enobarbus *there is no humor in the situation* as far as Antony's relation to Cleopatra and his neglect of his real opportunities are concerned.

Some Weaknesses in Criticism
of the Play

A DEPLORABLE weakness in much criticism of *Antony and Cleopatra* is the tendency of critics to withdraw lines and passages from context and cite them as evidence to support preconceived theories. For instance, the first conversation between Antony and Cleopatra in the play (I. i.) is frequently misinterpreted, as in Stauffer's "At the very start we learn that 'There's beggary in the love that can be reckon'd' and that to set limits to the love of this noble pair requires the finding out of 'new heaven, new earth'" (*Shakespeare's World of Images,* p. 244); or as in J. Dover Wilson's edition of the play (Cambridge, 1950), p. xviii: ". . . when the lovers enter . . . , we learn from their lips that this same love is more spacious than 'the wide arch of the ranged empire,' more precious than kingdoms or the whole 'dungy earth,' and so boundless that it requires 'new heaven, new earth' to contain it." That is hardly correct; what we really learn is that Antony is head over heels in love and wildly extravagant in his protestations and that Cleopatra is teasing and taunting him unmercifully.

Cleopatra's appearance is described by Griffiths (p. 40) thus: "She is represented by Shakespeare as at the extreme limit of the thirty-eight years Plutarch gives her at her death, her lip is waned, she is wrinkled deep in time, has a tawny front, is sunburnt," without regard to speaker in the play or circumstances. The "wan'd lip" is in a wish of Pompey's (II. i. 21); the "wrinkled deep in time" (I. v. 29) and the "sunburnt"—"with Phoebus' amorous pinches black" (I. v. 28)—are from Cleopatra's own self-pitying description, and the "tawny front" (I. i. 6) is Philo's scornful punning characterization. In each instance there are reasons for exaggeration or depreciation; it is illogical to put the details together as an objectively correct picture.

William Rosen in his *Shakespeare and the Craft of Tragedy* (Cambridge, Mass., 1960), pp. 124-125, likewise errs: "And like the world's greatest lovers who obliterate logic in the endeavor to achieve through love a transcendental state that defies ordinary human standards, Cleopatra describes her experience with Antony as beyond time and change, associated with all that is perfect and infinite:

> Eternity was in our lips and eyes,
> Bliss in our brows' bent, none our parts so poor
> But was a race of heaven.
>
> (I. iii. 35-37)

Actually Cleopatra is quoting what she says Antony said to her "When you su'd staying" (l. 33); those things you said, she says,

> are so still,
> Or thou, the greatest soldier of the world
> Art turn'd the greatest liar.

Cleopatra is not ecstatically describing "a transcendental state that defies ordinary human standards"; she is accusing Antony of "mouth-made vows/Which break themselves in swearing" (ll. 30-31). Here it is the critic, not Cleopatra, who obliterates logic.

A similar disregard of context appears in Harold Goddard's *The Meaning of Shakespeare* (Chicago, 1951), p. 582: "And so when Cleopatra, about to part from Antony, exclaims,

> Eternity was in our lips and eyes,
> Bliss in our brows, bent; none our parts so poor
> But was a race of heaven,

[65]

it strikes us less as affectation of divinity than as genuine perception of the divine element in love—insight into the heart of
something which their wildest words about each other are abortive
or rapturous attempts to express."

Likewise the statement by Farnham (p. 187), "when . . . he
[Antony] has had an opportunity to talk with the soothsayer,"
is misleading. Antony did not seek "an opportunity"; the
Soothsayer took advantage of an opportunity to confront Antony.
Similar assumptions about Antony and the Soothsayer are posited
by other critics.

If one were to make a thorough analysis of weaknesses in the
criticism of the play he would need to examine the unwarranted
use of Plutarch to substantiate opinions expressed. A particular
example is the assumption sometimes made that Plutarch ex-
plains the motive behind the Seleucus incident; Plutarch says:
"Caesar was glad to hear her say so [about gifts reserved for
Octavia and Livia and others], persuading himself thereby that
she had yet a desire to save her life." Shakespeare omits that
and thereby leaves the whole Seleucus incident a completely
unanswered question. Unless Shakespeare definitely utilizes a
statement by Plutarch, one must not cite such a statement as
evidence in the play.